Look, Ma! No Hands!

Life's Lessons Learned the Hard Way

Doe Hentschel

Green Heart Living Press

Look, Ma! No Hands!: Life's Lessons Learned the Hard Way
Copyright © 2022 Doe Hentschel

All rights reserved. No part of this book may be used or reproduced by any means, graphic, electronic, or mechanical, including photocopying, recording, taping or by any information storage retrieval system without the written permission of the publisher, except in the case of brief quotations embodied in critical articles and reviews.

ISBN Paperback: 978-1-954493-35-3

Cover design: Barb Pritchard, Infinity Brand Designs

This book is designed to provide information and motivation to our readers. It is sold with the understanding that the publisher is not engaged to render any type of psychological, legal, or any other kind of professional advice. The content of each article is the sole expression and opinion of its author, and not necessarily that of the publisher. No warranties or guarantees are expressed or implied by the publisher's choice to include any of the content in this volume. Neither the publisher nor the author shall be liable for any physical, psychological, emotional, financial, or commercial damages, including, but not limited to, special, incidental, consequential or other damages. Our views and rights are the same: You are responsible for your own choices, actions, and results.

Dedication

*This book is dedicated to my angels
who give me opportunities to learn and grow,
and to my butterflies
who tell me I am ready.*

This book would not exist without them in my life.

Contents

Foreword	7
Preface	9
Chapter 1: What Kind of Doctor Are You?	13
Chapter 2: Is It My Fault?	19
Chapter 3: Write It on the Wall	27
Chapter 4: The Nurses Are in Charge	33
Chapter 5: The Helpers	39
Chapter 6: What Smells?	45
Chapter 7: Progressing from Bad to Worse	51
Chapter 8: Ten Times Bigger	59
Chapter 9: Tissues, Butterscotch, Hinges and Turnbuckles	67
Chapter 10: About Barricades	73
Chapter 11: Delusions and Train Wrecks	81
Chapter 12: Puzzle Pieces	85
Epilogue	99
Acknowledgements and Gratitude	101
Books Referenced	109
About the Author	113
About the Illustrator	115

Foreword

Rarely in our lives do we meet someone whom we recognize immediately to be a beacon—a beacon of light, love and hope. When I met Doe in 2009 and gave her the life-altering diagnosis of Parkinson's disease, I knew she was such a one. And this lovely book, *Look, Ma! No Hands*! epitomizes all that she embodies in actual life. Here, she shares stories that are charming, humorous and deeply insightful in a style that is uniquely hers. It is the "Dose of Doe" that I have been begging her to bottle for me for years—a dose of her optimism, strength of character, wisdom, and that almost whimsical resilience that makes her simply indefatigable! This may not be in a bottle, but this book is definitely the Dose of Doe that I have wanted to share with so many of my other patients throughout my career. We are blessed.

J. Antonelle de Marcaida, M.D.
Associate Clinical Professor of Neurology
Medical Director, Hartford HealthCare's Chase Family Movement Disorders Center

Preface

The asphalt was warm…not hot like it would have been earlier in the afternoon, just toasty warm having absorbed hours of July's heat. It was rough under my calves, hotter and sharp under my heels. The stench of burned rubber mixed with the scent of my own sweat. I breathed in deeply and felt a stabbing pain in my chest.

My heart pounded in my ears, drowning out the sounds of footsteps running. I opened my eyes and was blinded by the setting sun. *Red sky at night.* I closed them again and tried another breath; the knife struck again. *Sailor's delight.* A car door slammed, shattering the near silence surrounding me. A firm but gentle hand touched my cheek.

"Don't move," he said. "I'm an EMT." I opened my eyes again. His face blocked the glare of the sun and I saw the others, crowded close around me, wide eyed, motionless. "Where does it hurt?"

"My chest."

He moved his hand, carefully pressing against my ribs. "Tell me where." A siren wailed in the distance, coming closer.

"Higher, under the sternum."

He paused; his questioning eyes met mine. "Do you have medical knowledge?"

"No," I took a shallow breath, hoping to soften the stab, "I'm just smart."

Weeks later when the puzzled people who did have medical knowledge questioned how I could possibly have shattered both elbows simultaneously when the force was obviously directed from my midsection (under the sternum) outward to the elbows, I had no answer.

"Well, I'm not going to show you, that's for sure!" So much for smart.

The short answer was simply that I had smashed my bike—make that my daughter's bike, a 10-speed I'd never ridden before and that neither she nor I would ever ride again—into a moving automobile, broadside. It was the start of yet another "fitness" campaign, and having discovered that when I tried to run, my legs got tired, I decided to strengthen them by bicycling.

Karin's red Schwinn was hanging on hooks in our garage; my friend Ray checked the tires to be sure they were inflated; and while he ran, I biked. It didn't take long for him to far outdistance me, but as he turned a corner and headed downhill on a newly paved street, I (being smart) decided I could catch him by the time he reached the cross street just half a block from my house. After all, I know the law of gravity means you go fast with less effort when you're going down hill, and I never even took physics!

But this car got in the way. As I raced toward the intersection I saw that a rusty, old, brown jalopy was also entering the intersection, perpendicular to my direction (I did take geometry). It wasn't going very fast and obviously wasn't going to get out of my way in time and the wind was whistling in my ears and I grabbed the handbrakes and squeezed...hard and fast. Not smart. The bike stopped alright, and I didn't.

Preface

For the next six months I had no hands, at least no functional hands, or arms. My shattered elbows were reset and placed in casts at 45 degree angles, hands crossed over my sternum (aka breastbone). The initial treatment, removing the radial head—that's one of three bones in the joint—in the left elbow, resulted in the left elbow healing in a dislocated position (yes, I sued him).

Subsequent surgery that included installing pins to hold the joint together while it healed, also failed to create stability in that arm. More surgeries at the Mayo Clinic, by the man who wrote the book on elbows, and spending more than two years 24-7 in bilateral splints finally gave me the use of my arms again…not full motion but enough to do everything I need to do.

This book is not about my accident or my injuries or my medical treatment. I've told you most of what you really need to know about that. It is, rather, about the lessons I learned during that six-month period when I, for the most part, had no hands. I've waited to write it for many years; and I continue to learn about myself, about others, and about life as I reflect upon those six months.

Perhaps my stories, and the lessons I have drawn from them, will have as much meaning for you as they have for me. And maybe bring a smile to your face and make you chuckle a bit. I do.

Chapter 1

What Kind of Doctor Are You?

Monday July 21, 1986 11 p.m.

"I'm glad to see you're awake, Dolores."

"Please call me Doe."

The nurse smiled, "What a beautiful name."

"I made it up."

I never liked "Dolores" even though my parents thought it would be a beautiful name for the little girl they had brought into the world, who, they told me, they expected to look like a Spanish beauty—with dark eyes and an olive complexion like theirs. Never mind that they weren't Spanish. Mother's heritage was German and Danish and Daddy's was Polish or Lithuanian, depending on which family historian you believe.

I don't know if Mother also knew that in Spanish cultures mothers sometimes name their daughters "Dolores" to remind them of the pain they suffered bringing their daughters into the world. She certainly did remember the pain. I knew from childhood that she had labored for 24 hours before I made my entrance, fair-skinned, blue-eyed with a fuzz of pale yellow that didn't grow for more than two years.

When she arrived home with my baby brother 22 months later (who did have their darker skin tone—beet red at birth—complemented by jet black eyes and long stringy black hair), she tucked me in and listened to my prayers.

"God bless Mommy, God bless Daddy, God bless Keith-y, God bless Lorie."

"Who's Lorie?" she asked.

"That's me."

For years when she told this story she would explain that at not-quite-two I couldn't pronounce "Dolores," even though she also bragged about my articulation even at that early age. "The only word you ever mispronounced was 'ice-a-preem' and I never corrected you because I figured a two-year-old could mispronounce one word."

I didn't mispronounce "Dolores"; I renamed myself "Lorie."

As far as I know, no one but Auntie Madge, who was living with us then while Uncle Bud was on a battleship in the Pacific, ever called me Lorie. I loved getting birthday cards from her. Even when I was an adult, they always included a note that started out, "Dear Lorie." I often thought if we could choose our mothers, I would have chosen Auntie Madge.

In eighth grade I decided I'd had enough of "Dolores" and called myself "DoDo." It caught on with my friends, and I even ran for class treasurer with posters all over the school urging my peers to "Let DoDo keep the money." I didn't get elected, but worse than that my friends were asking if we'd changed our telephone number because they kept getting the wrong number when they called. Then I caught Mother in the act!

"I'm sorry; you must have the wrong number. No one by that name lives here."

"Who was that call for?" I asked.

"It was the wrong number. They wanted someone named DoDo."

"That's me!" I declared.

"Not while you live in this house!"

Sometimes I guess mothers do know things...

So, I called a meeting. Sybil and Sandi and Susie and I put our heads together in the cafeteria to find me a new name.

"Why don't you call yourself 'Doe,' like a deer?" suggested Sybil. I've been "Doe" ever since. Happily, even Mother acquiesced, and my social life got back on track in no time.

"Would you like some water, Doe? The doctor just called to put you on NPO because he's scheduled surgery for you tomorrow."

Her question brought me back to the present, to the sterile and barren surrounds of my hospital bed. My mind felt like it was moving in slow motion as I processed the night nurse's statement. I wasn't supposed to have surgery. I'd had x-rays when the ambulance brought me to the hospital the night before and more x-rays this morning. The doctor had told me I didn't need surgery; I was sure of it.

"There's a mistake," I told the nurse. "He told me I didn't need surgery."

"Well, I guess he's changed his mind; he just called and you are scheduled for the morning."

He appeared at my bedside with a colleague in tow early in the morning. They explained that there were bone chips in the left elbow which needed to be removed, and that the radial head was splintered and not able to work the way it needed to in the elbow joint. So, they wanted to remove it.

"Do you put in something to replace it?" I asked.

"No, the body will accommodate for it being gone."

I'd heard that before. When there was a drain in my abdomen after my gallbladder was removed, they pulled out the drain and the hole just closed up...no stitches were needed. That doctor told me my "body would accommodate." It did.

"What kind of a doctor are you?" I inquired...maybe about 36 hours too late.

"A surgeon."

"You mean, a general surgeon, like one who takes out an appendix?"

"Yes."

I turned to his buddy. "And what kind of doctor are you?"

"A surgeon."

"Well, if we're talking about taking out part of one of my bones, I want to see an orthopedic surgeon."

It turns out there were no orthopedic surgeons on the staff of this tiny community hospital just two minutes by ambulance from my home. There were three who had privileges there, and at my insistence they were called. One was on vacation, one was leaving on vacation the next day (after all, it was July and people aren't supposed to ram their bikes into moving cars in the middle of the summer!), and the third told the surgeon that I could make an appointment in his office in a week. The pain in my elbow screeched—*A WEEK???*

"What other option is there?" I asked, thinking how different a radial head is from an appendix.

"Well, we could put you in an ambulance and take you to another hospital and see if there is an orthopedic surgeon who will take your case."

What a great plan. Load me up like a bag of bricks, roll me down the hall, into an ambulance that will hit every pothole left over from winter, screech around every corner, and drive around for hours while they wheel my cart into every hospital in the metropolitan area until we find some bone doctor who isn't going on vacation and who has the time to see me now and not next week and figure out what to do about this unbearable pain that seems to be unaffected by these pills they keep putting down my throat.

"You are telling me that this pain is because this bone won't go back in place?"

"Yes."

"And it won't go back in place because it is splintered, and there are bone chips in there?"

"Yes."

"And if we don't take out this bone, I'll have an arthritic elbow?"

"Yes."

"Then do the surgery."

Look, Ma! No Hands!

Lessons learned: No matter how much it hurts, ask questions. Even if you are pretty smart, ask someone who has medical knowledge if you asked the right questions and whether the answers you got make sense.

Chapter 2

Is It My Fault?

Monday, January 25, 1988 10 a.m.

Fast forward 18 months. One of Rochester's famous blizzards is predicted to begin this afternoon just in time to snarl rush hour traffic. The taxi drops me off at the hospital entrance. The first time Karin and I came here to meet Ann was after I moved to New York in 1982. The long hallway in the entrance of the old Victorian building, now converted into a wing of professional offices, is just as cavernous as I recalled.

My footsteps echoed as I walked toward her office. I hadn't noticed how dark and gloomy that hallway was then; maybe it was just the winter light, or lack thereof, in this city with so few sunny days.

I passed the bench where I'd sat waiting during that first visit while she talked with my 13-year-old daughter. A colleague at the university had referred me to Ann when I told her that I thought Karin might need some help dealing with her father Tom's and my separation, the conflict over whether she could move to New York with me or stay with her father and older brother Brian, and the move.

Ann met with us together, then with Karin alone and with me alone. She agreed that it would be helpful for Karin to spend some time with her and suggested that I would also benefit from sessions with her. Karin "graduated" after three sessions and Ann assured me that she was not likely to grow up hating men or me.

I, on the other hand, spent six months in weekly sessions with this remarkable and talented woman who had a gift for helping me reexamine the puzzle of the life I was creating—consider pieces of the puzzle that did not fit in the emerging picture I was creating as a forty-year-old, single, professional woman. She skillfully helped me describe with more clarity what I was looking for to fill in new patterns in this picture I had not intended to create two decades earlier.

She was quiet. She listened a lot and interjected pointed, specific questions at just the right moment as I studied a piece that I thought was key to the whole picture. We would examine it together: Where did it come from, what did it connect to years ago, will it still fit? If not, will there be a blank spot…a hole in this new picture?

If I still needed it, will it connect in a different way to other pieces, some of which are new? Or, alternatively, is it time to get rid of it all together? The process I had been using for 40 years to create this puzzle had been disrupted. The old picture didn't work any more, but I was not starting from scratch as I tried to

Is It My Fault?

redesign this puzzle with no picture on the front of a box to guide me. It was taking a long time for this hard work.

"You're very good at this," she complimented me one day.

"Me?" I was incredulous. "You're the therapist. I've worked with many different people for the last 15 years—in and out of marriage counseling and working on myself as well. In fact, I think I'm something of a connoisseur of counselors! I know a good one.

"It's kind of like riding a bike...if you climb on and push the pedals but don't go anywhere, you know it's not a real bike but a stationary one. You can move your body a lot but you don't get to a different place. A good counselor gets that bike off the blocks, and while it's hard work moving it uphill, you eventually reach that place where it's smooth sailing, fast coasting downhill and you're at a new destination.

"That's what you do for me—encourage me to keep pedaling; and when we reach that pinnacle, you smile as I race forward."

"Interesting analogy." She smiled softly. "Who is doing the pedaling?"

So, here I am again six years later, settling into the squooshy sofa in her warm, inviting office—so different from the cold and barren hallway leading to it. I had called her from Connecticut, where I moved just eight weeks after that other bike ride in 1986, because I needed help.

"I'll block out the day for you, Doe. If we work hard, we can do in one day what would take others months."

She looked at the splints on my arms, jointed with metal hinges and taped on with Velcro strips. Turnbuckles perched on top of both arms, connecting the forearms and the upper arms and applying constant pressure to stretch the joints. The goal was to regain mobility.

"Those are quite the contraptions!"

"I'm known as the bionic dean," I smiled. "I'm suing the doctor who first treated me. After surgery he never x-rayed and didn't even know the left elbow had healed in a dislocated position. We're tying to fix that now with these splints."

"And why are you here?"

"I feel like it's really my fault."

Five hours later I walked down that corridor again and into the snow that had started right on cue. The cab driver got out, opened the door for me (my splinted arms hidden under the heavy woolen winter cape I wore) and drove slowly toward the airport.

"Hope your flight doesn't get canceled."

Monday, March 20, 1989 4 p.m.

I was putting the last things into my suitcase, preparing to leave the following afternoon for my court date in Rochester. Months of investigation and depositions were about to culminate in the federal court. I remembered the accident, the ride to the hospital, sirens screaming in my ears, the pain now radiating from the sternum to my upper arms. Excruciating pain. I wanted to scream.

Is It My Fault?

I remembered being wheeled into x-ray again the next morning when they took my arms out of the casts and straightened them again for more pictures. This time I did scream, and the nurse accompanying me said she was surprised I didn't pass out.

I remembered asking for an orthopedic surgeon, weeks of continued pain unrelieved by opiates that others put in my mouth, repeated questions about when I would start physical therapy and then another opinion, more surgery, and more…I remembered it all too well. The phone interrupted my reverie.

"They've offered a settlement." It was my lawyer in Rochester. We'd never talked about money except when he told me only one in ten malpractice cases is decided in favor of the plaintiff in Monroe County and that the average settlement in those cases was $30,000. "It's $250,000."

I breathed deeply. No stab in my chest, but a big lump in my throat.

"I need to think about this."

"Of course," he reassured me. "But you need to know this is their second offer. I turned down the first."

"It's not about the money," I said. "I need to be sure that I don't feel that I'm abdicating my own responsibility here. For a long time I felt that way about this whole situation, and I need to feel okay now."

I called him back before breakfast. "I'll take the settlement." There was a long pause.

"Are you sure?"

"Yes I am."

"I'm surprised. I've been in this business for a long time, and people enter into these negligence and malpractice cases for different reasons. For some it's the money, but for most it's something else. I thought for you it was that you need to tell your story…for others to know he was wrong."

"Well, you are partly right. I need for *him* to know he was wrong; that he had no business treating me after they saw that first x-ray; that he should have put me back in the ambulance right then and sent me to the closest major medical center—15 minutes away; that he was on probation for a reason; that he didn't answer my questions honestly or give me real choices—all for a $9000 operation.

"This offer makes it clear he does know he was wrong, or at least his insurance company does. I don't need to relive it in public; I don't need to open up this anger and hurt and resentment. I can close the book knowing that I was taken advantage of—abused. And it wasn't my fault. If I'd been in a coma, he had no right…"

Then I called Ann.

"I've settled. I'm okay. Thank you."

Is It My Fault?

Lessons learned: Accidents happen. It's not abdicating your responsibility for decision making when those who are entrusted with your care do you harm.

When you have no medical knowledge, those who do must use it ethically and wisely. It's not your fault if they don't, no matter how responsible and smart you are.

Chapter 3

Write It on the Wall

July 26, 1986 10:00 a.m.

"Can you get a big roll of newsprint and tape it up in the hallway?" I asked Meg, the LPN whom I had hired to assist with my Aunt Dot for whom I was the caretaker. Meg was living with Karin and me this summer trying to save money to return to school to finish her bachelor's degree. "I want to keep track of things I can do with no hands."

Meg laughed. "Well, right now that's a pretty short list," she said. "But I'll get the newsprint."

After five days in the hospital, I had come home; and Karin, Meg, Tom, and I became a decision-making team charged with transforming my house to accommodate my limitations. Tom had come from Chicago to support Karin and me during the traumatic time following the accident.

We immediately realized that I could not sleep in my own bed—a king-size waterbed recommended years before because of my back problems. I simply could not get in and out of that bed without the use of my arms. The living room with its sofa bed became my bedroom.

We also discovered that going up and down stairs was a challenge. My body's center of gravity was altered and I was often dizzy from the pain medication I needed. Obviously I couldn't hold on to the banister. The first floor powder room would suffice for toileting, although it was barely big enough to accommodate two people. I know you are wondering—you cannot go to the bathroom alone with no hands! We knew we would need to figure out a way to convert one of the upstairs bathrooms for bathing. This would of course require that I would be accompanied on the stairs by helpers acting like "spotters" on belays at a ropes course and would have to be bathed by someone else.

Tom and Karin went shopping for attire that I could wear given that my arms were basically strapped to my torso, making it impossible to put my arms in sleeves. They returned with several maternity mumus—large enough to slip over my head (someone else had to do that, of course) and full enough to cover my enlarged midriff. Maternity worked. I looked like a jack-in-the-box, head sticking out of a fuchsia balloon. Lovely.

Realizing the things I could not do became depressing and scary. I had had enough by the time Meg returned with the newsprint, masking tape to affix it to the hall wall, and markers that she tested to be sure they would not bleed through.

"I can laugh. Please write that in big bold letters," I directed.

Meg complied. "You can also cry, Doe," she added.

"Nope. Can't cry," I retorted.

"It's okay to cry. This is serious stuff, Doe. You don't have to be brave 24/7…it's okay to cry."

"Wrong! When I cry, my nose starts to run and then someone comes at me with a Kleenex and smashes it up against my nose. I feel like I'm being suffocated! Now I know why toddlers run the other direction and would rather eat their snot than have someone wipe their nose! No crying."

As the days went by and we settled into a routine, we discovered other things I could do. I could lick my pain pills off the counter! The pain in my left elbow continued unabated. It was exacerbated by a painful right shoulder that had separated in the accident. It was in a sling that applied pressure with the goal of coaching the separation to bond again (or something like that—whatever it was, it didn't work).

We learned that a pain pill every four hours was needed to bring the pain down to at least a tolerable level, but that was around the clock. Provided someone else put the pill on the counter, filled a glass of water and put a bending straw in it, I could get up for that "middle of the night" dose, lick my pain pill off the counter and then go back to my sofa bed without disturbing anyone else.

I (and I suspect they) were relieved to know they could sleep through the night and wake up refreshed and alert enough to do all the other things I needed help with during the daytime and evening hours. *Write that on the wall!*

When friends came to visit, we often brainstormed new items to add to the slowly expanding list.

"You can dance," said Jill.

"Not too fast," added my more cautious friend, Mary.

"You can talk on the phone…as long as someone else dials the number and holds the receiver to your ear." (There were no such things as speaker phones in 1986, and we really did dial the numbers.)

I could read, and eventually figured out how to turn the pages by myself! And as I got more skilled with manipulating small items with the tips of my fingers that extended beyond the ends of the casts on both arms, I could turn on the lights!

The suggestion that I could tell stories was shot down by Dema.

"Doe can't possibly tell stories with no hands! She gestures all the time—that's her natural style."

Knowing that isolation is the worst punishment in the world for me, as soon as I was strong enough to venture out, friends would take me out for lunch or dinner. They would, of course, have to feed me, but I conquered my embarrassment at being so dependent in public and enjoyed these outings immensely. The discomfort from the constant pressure on my shoulder made sitting up for more than about an hour difficult, so we would eat and get me home within a pretty narrow time frame.

After returning home one evening, my friends joined me in the living room so I could lie down on my sofa bed and we could continue the visit. I launched into a story about a pet parakeet I once had and began to describe the tall, circular cage she liked to sit atop as soon as I opened it in the morning. As I began to illustrate the shape of this unusual cage with my feet, Dema jumped up, grabbed a marker and ran to the hall.

"Doe CAN tell stories," she announced!

Years later as I was reminiscing about those challenging weeks, I recalled that another item on the list was that I could make my bed with my toes. I had quite a system for straightening the bedclothes by grabbing them with my toes and pulling them up and then smoothing them out for a passable "made bed." It wouldn't have passed inspection in the military or even a Motel 6, but it was good enough and made it possible for me to "entertain" in my living room without feeling I was inviting people into the bedroom.

As I told this story, Valerie asked, "Why would you do that? Surely someone else would have been happy to make the bed for you!"

I thought for a moment. She was right. I was surrounded by helpers who happily did everything that needed to be done, but it was important for me to do it myself.

"I did it because I could."

The experience of having such a severe limitation that so greatly impacted my independence helped me to understand my friend Will's tenacity. Will's childhood polio had resulted in his dependence on crutches, but he would do things himself, even when it would have been easy for me to do these things for him. I would grimace with projected discomfort as he would laboriously get up from his desk, cross the office to retrieve something from the bookcase that I could easily and quickly have brought to him. "I'll do it," he would say. Now I understand.

Lessons learned: Focus on the positive and celebrate your skills. There are lots of things that you cannot do, but that does not mean you are helpless. And when those around you struggle to assert their independence and abilities, respect their need to "do it themselves," even if they need to ask you to write it on their wall for them.

Chapter 4

The Nurses Are in Charge

July 26, 1986 2:00 p.m.

Karin dialed the phone and held it to my ear so I could break the news to Terry that our vacation was off.

Ten days before I raced down that hill into the jalopy, I had accepted a new job as Dean of Extended and Continuing Education at the University of Connecticut. Scheduled to begin at the end of August after transporting Karin to begin her freshman year at college in Florida, I had planned a trip the last week in July to Connecticut to find housing. A longtime friend from Chicago was planning to go with me. Terry had never been to New England, and we were looking forward to house hunting during a long-overdue reunion exploring the state that would soon be my home.

And then I smashed my elbows.

"Obviously, this trip isn't going to happen," I explained. "I cannot travel right now, and I'm going to have to find housing some other way. I hope you can figure out a way to get a refund on your airline ticket."

There was a long pause. "Not on your life would I cancel this trip, Doe. I can visit New England any time, but when else would I have ten days to wipe your bottom?" Terry, a nurse, had immediately grasped the nitty-gritty details of my situation!

And so it evolved that the day Karin flew to Chicago with her dad to spend her own two-week vacation with him and Brian, Terry arrived prepared to share nursing duty with Meg. The two of them sat at the kitchen table over coffee after dinner that first night, discussed my care and divided up the tasks as if I were not there!

"We've got a pretty good routine," Meg explained. "Doe can get through the night alone, and even though she wakes up early, she doesn't mind waiting for breakfast. Karin and I aren't morning people, so breakfast is usually about 9:30 or 10."

"Well, that won't change," Terry replied. "I'm not a morning person either! Let's just alternate the morning shift. So, when does she get bathed? At night or after breakfast?"

The answer was "after breakfast," and the next morning was Terry's turn. She came downstairs about nine and was surprised to see that I had made my bed (with my toes). Having licked my morning pain pill off the counter, I was sitting at the kitchen table ready for breakfast. She put on a pot of coffee and fixed and fed me scrambled eggs and toast while we reminisced and did more catching up on the years since we had seen each other.

Terry and her husband lived one floor above Tom and me when we both brought our baby boys into the world ten days apart. Brian was the littlest baby I had ever seen, weighing in at 6 pounds ¾ oz, but Christopher looked like a little Buddha on day one.

Brian was as active after birth as he was in utero and apparently wasn't aware of the "fact" that newborns sleep most of the day, wake up only to be fed and then go back to sleep. Christopher was the baby they wrote that chapter about. At three weeks, Brian settled into a daily routine that included shrieking in pain from 4:00 in the afternoon until settling down about midnight for two or three hours of sleep. The books identified this pattern as "colic," and nothing the books suggested did much to calm him. Thanks to the quality of construction in our apartment building, Terry could hear his cries and became familiar with the path I walked in the living room patting his back trying to comfort him.

One day about 4:30 in the afternoon, there was a knock on the door. It was Terry.

"Let's trade babies for a while." Christopher was asleep (of course), and I went upstairs while Terry cradled Brian on her shoulder and began patting and pacing. Several times a week we traded babies until Brian's gastro-intestinal system relaxed, and Terry and I had been there for each other ever since.

"OK," Terry said after her second cup of coffee (I don't drink it), "let's do the shower thing!"

The "shower thing" was no small thing. After experimenting with a variety of techniques, what was finally working pretty well once I successfully mastered the challenge of climbing the stairs, was to cover my body with a gigantic trash bag to prevent the casts on my arms from getting wet. This in and of itself was a challenge. A hole had to be cut in the bottom of the bag for my head, and the bag was then lowered to envelop my torso. Picture a hand puppet in a nondescript black gown. Cute. Not.

We had found a metal porch chair that fit in the tub, and the hand-held shower head made it possible to direct the water (carefully so that it didn't get inside the bag from the neck opening) to rinse my various body parts after soaping with a washcloth. Terry got the bag on me, helped me step into the tub and sit on the chair, and with feedback from me, got the right water temperature. She moistened a washcloth and began to wash my face.

"Meg does my bottom first," I told her. "Then after she finishes below the waist, she does my face." Terry stopped. Long pause. A frown.

"Doe, let's get one thing straight. The nurses do NOT want to hear how the other nurses do it. Not ever." I was effectively silenced and she continued washing my face. She then soaped up the washcloth, lifted the bottom of the bag and started moving south. A few inches later, she paused.

"So Meg does the bottom first, and then washes your face with the washcloth?"

Nonplussed, I responded, "Well, she uses a new washcloth."

"Not anymore! The laundry is now one of *my* jobs. One washcloth per shower is the new rule!"

Terry's admonition quite probably contributed to the sustainability of the vast support network I would need for the next two years. People who washed my body, brushed my teeth, shampooed my hair, applied my make-up, dressed me, cleaned my house, stacked the dishwasher, put away the groceries, fixed my meals, and did many other things I could not do for myself had their own ways of doing things.

I never would have believed anyone would brush their teeth with warm water, but some people do; and when they wanted to brush mine with warm water, I recognized that the end result was just fine even if it felt a bit weird! I even discovered that some of the new hairdos I sported were quite attractive and that there were places in my house that I never even knew needed to be cleaned that now sparkled!

Lessons learned: There's always more than one way to do almost anything, and people like to do it their own way. If you want or need help, be grateful for however it gets done. And, if you are cleaning up a mess, it might be a good idea to start at the top, especially if you are the one who does the laundry.

Chapter 5

The Helpers

July 28, 1986 4:00 p.m.

Gladys stopped in to visit one day after work. "I've been thinking," she said. "I go right by the supermarket on my way home from work, and your house is in between. Why don't I call every day before I leave the office and find out if you need anything? That way, Karin or Meg won't have to leave you alone to do major grocery shopping very often."

What a great idea that turned out to be! Meg got a stash of cash from my bank account, and we kept a running list of needs. Almost every day, Gladys would drop off the needed supplies, get reimbursed, and be on her way.

Barbara had a different idea. "Doe, I would love to visit, but the last thing you need during the day is for me and Tommy to descend on your house." Tommy, an active…maybe hyperactive… toddler, had little interest in spending quiet time in a convalescent's home! "However, I could come in the evenings after Kenny is home to be with Tommy, and if you are comfortable with my helping with your paperwork, bills, etc., you know that's in my skill set."

"Are you kidding? You would do that?" Handling the mail and all the accompanying tasks that go with it can be daunting any time. "Handling the mail" was not listed on the wall of "things Doe can do with no hands."

I was preparing to move, so the paperwork included closing accounts, changing addresses, and what seemed like an insurmountable pile of other things that needed hands to get done. Barbara, whose pre-motherhood career was as a bookkeeper, came over two nights a week to ensure that my credit rating didn't suffer, the utilities didn't get turned off before the move, and once I knew the location of my new home, make sure everyone would be able to find me in Connecticut.

"What are all those stacks of newspapers in the garage?" Ray asked. "You must have three years of newspapers in there."

"Four years, actually," I admitted. "I hate to throw them out, and this town doesn't recycle. I never found a place to take them."

The next weekend, Ray and two buddies arrived with a pickup truck that they filled twice with four years worth of newspapers and delivered them to a recycling center in a nearby town.

Penny anticipated yet another task necessitated by my upcoming move. "I am really good at throwing things out," she announced. She and I spent several afternoons spread over several weeks going through one closet at a time, one dresser at a time, the bookshelves and the basement.

We made three piles: "Connecticut," "Church Rummage Sale," "Who needs this anyway? Trash." Each day, she would load up her car with the rummage sale stack, put the trash out at the curb, and neatly replace the things destined to make the move with me to facilitate the packing that would precede the actual move.

The timing of the move, of course, needed to be reconsidered. My original plan had been to begin my new duties before Labor Day immediately after getting Karin settled in her dormitory in late August. Tom stepped up and offered to drive from Chicago, pick up Karin and drive her to her college in Florida where they would spend several days buying the paraphernalia she would need and otherwise get her settled in. My superiors at UConn were very supportive after getting over the shock of my accident and subsequent injuries, and the start date was now scheduled to be September 15.

I did need to find a place to move to! I called Beverly, the dean's administrative assistant, and asked if there was any university housing that might be available, at least temporarily. While the university does own a number of houses which are rented to faculty and staff, she learned that none were available for September. She discouraged me from considering any of the local apartment complexes unless I would find it enjoyable to be surrounded by undergraduates who appear to sleep more during class than at night and who begin their weekends on Thursday afternoons. Scratch that.

Beverly asked what my requirements were, the most challenging being a living room large enough for the baby grand piano that a boyfriend and I had purchased together. When he became my ex-boyfriend, he had no money to "buy me out," so the piano became mine. I had thought that I might finally indulge myself with piano lessons when Karin went to college and I would have slightly more free time.

But then I smashed my elbows...

A few days later, Beverly called back with great news. A friend of hers was moving out of state and was interested in renting her townhouse in the suburb where Beverly lived. It was a short 25-minute commute to the university and it had a big living room. Perfect. I rented it sight unseen over the phone.

Beverly asked if I had a doctor yet, and of course I did not. She referred me to an orthopedic surgeon in the same town which also conveniently had a fine hospital with a well respected physical therapy department. A telephone call with Dr. Jacobsen, who was quite intrigued to learn I had bilateral comminuted fractures of the elbows (an injury he told me was impossible to incur), secured an appointment on September 12.

Dorothy came for lunch one day. When I had reorganized my unit at the college and needed a new administrative assistant, Dorothy was the obvious choice. She was ready for a new challenge at the college and her experience was invaluable to me, the tenth dean of continuing education in ten years! She knew the players and the potholes, the policies and the procedures. I liked her a lot. She kept me organized, made sure I was always prepared for meetings, took the initiative to solve problems and contributed in many other ways to making sure the eleventh dean would not be needed for several more years.

The Helpers

As she fed me the fifth salad I had had that week, she laid out a plan.

"We've been talking about moving you." She did not identify the antecedent of "we," but it soon became clear. "Your house closing is on Wednesday, the 10th and since the buyer has agreed not to take possession until the 12th, we figure the packing could be done on the 10th, the movers could come on the 11th and deliver everything to your townhouse on the 12th.

"Meg will drive you to Connecticut after they load up the truck; the two of you can check out the townhouse and spend that night in a nearby hotel, and you can meet the movers at the townhouse the next morning. They'll unload and unpack while Meg takes you to meet with Dr. Jacobsen, and that night you should be able to sleep in your new house!

"Saturday, the 13th, Meg will drive to the airport, meet me at my plane, tell me where your car is parked and then she will fly home. I'll spend the next three weeks with you to get you settled, open your bank accounts, get your insurance policies, license plates, etc. And I will hire someone to drive you to work and provide assistance."

"Dorothy, I can't ask you to do that!"

"You didn't."

"Well, how can you take three weeks off work?"

She laughed. "I have a very healthy bank of vacation days; you should know that!"

"Yes, but I can't let you use your vacation days doing this."

"Excuse me," she was serious as she put another forkful of lettuce in my mouth. "You are not my boss anymore."

Lessons learned: There are times when you do need help. When people tell you exactly what they can do to help, it's much easier to accept that assistance. Remember that when someone you know needs help, even if that someone used to be your boss.

Chapter 6
What Smells?

August 14, 1986 3:00 p.m.

"Something smells really bad in here," I announced to Karin when she came home from running errands. Before leaving, she had gotten me settled on the couch in the family room, where I was lying on my back. Sitting up was still quite painful because of the pressure on my separated shoulder. *And Ladies of the Club* was propped up on my chest at just the right distance from my eyes so I could read the small type on its 1,176 pages and turn the pages with the tips of my fingers.

I'd bought this highly acclaimed historical novel when it had achieved notoriety as the work of an elderly woman who had died before knowing that the book had become wildly popular. Although she had begun writing it decades earlier, she had not had time to complete writing it until she became very old and moved into a nursing home.

Having bought it before realizing how long this tome was, I had set it aside because I did not have time to read 1,176 pages.

And then I smashed my elbows.

Now I had the time, and this book was so big and fat and heavy that it was the perfect book for right now. It sat squarely on my prone chest supported by its hard covers the perfect distance from my hands that were, of course, also crossed on my chest.

As I became engrossed in the goings on in post-civil war Waynesboro, I became distracted by an unpleasant odor I could not identify. I was sure it was not gas—a good thing, given that I had no idea how I would get...*the Ladies*...off my chest, get myself upright (the logistics involved in rising from the family room couch were significantly different than those needed to get up from the sofa bed in the living room) and evacuate the house before it exploded. Door handles were impossible to manipulate and, of course, calling 911 was an impossible task.

Continuing my olfactory analysis, I decided that this was not a chemical odor. It was not rotten eggs or sour milk, but it did seem to be something that was "spoiled." I turned a few more pages hoping that my nose would get bored with this nasty aroma. As the time went on, I became more and more annoyed at the length of time Karin was taking to complete errands I was sure should not have taken more than 30 minutes.

I began to consider that this might be the stench of death. I'd never smelled a dead body—human or otherwise—but this smell was surely that bad. Having decided that I was smelling something dead, I became nauseated and panicked that if I threw up, I would probably die choking on my own vomit. I could not, after all, get...*the Ladies*...off my chest, get myself upright, open a kitchen cupboard and grab a pot...or get to the toilet in time. I wondered how my demise would be described in my obituary. And then the door to the garage opened.

"Something smells really bad in here."
Karin sniffed. "I don't smell anything."
"You're too far away. Come over here."
She stepped closer and sniffed.
"Nope."
"Bend down, near my head."
She bent down.
"Whoa! Yuck! That's awful!"
"I told you so. I think it's something dead." She deftly took...*the Ladies*...off my chest, helped me get up and out of the way, and then removed the cushions.

"I bet Abner brought a creature in," she said as she searched the crevices in the couch. I was doubtful. Abner was the most docile cat we'd ever owned and had never demonstrated any interest in hunting. Our first cat, a calico named Ms, whom we adopted when our neighbors moved to London, was a hunter who brought something home every morning. Mice, moles, baby rabbits, birds...but of course we disposed of them before they smelled. Abner never brought anything home. I began to wonder where Abner was. I hadn't seen him in days.

"Good grief! Maybe it's Abner! Pull the couch out and check behind it."

Karin moved the couch. Nothing there. She pushed the couch back against the wall, replaced the cushions and looked as puzzled as I was feeling.

We walked into the kitchen together and suddenly Karin stopped.

"Mom, the odor moves with you. It's on you." She stepped closer and began sniffing. "AAACCCK!" She stopped the exploration at my armpit. "It IS you."

We began to laugh and to this day the memory of that discovery brings a grin to my face. Once we stopped laughing and Karin wiped the tears away that were rolling down my cheeks, the question of why my armpits smelled like dead rats required an answer. We realized that with all the careful and deliberate methodology that had been developed to bathe me (bag over head, wash the face first the lower body next), not once in the four weeks since I smashed my elbows had my underarms been washed! My arms were immobilized in casts along my torso, forearms at 45° angles facing up with my hands crossed in front of the sternum. There was no way to lift my arms for what we now realized was much-needed hygiene.

By trial and error, we solved the problem, and when Meg returned home that evening, Karin demonstrated the new protocol to be employed on a daily basis. after removing my garbage bag after my shower.

"After you take off the garbage bag and while the soap is still wet, you soap up this old toothbrush," she

What Smells?

explained to Meg. "Then you push it into Mom's armpit, like this, brush it back and forth a couple of times, then pull it out. Then take a washcloth (you need a new one since the shower washcloth did her bottom) get it nice and wet and push it through the armpit until you can pull it out from the back. You might have to do that a couple of times to get the soap off, and then use a dry washcloth to dry out the armpit. Then you do the same thing on the other side."

"So this is two MORE washcloths just for the armpits for every shower? Three washcloths all together?"

"You should have smelled her armpits."

"I'll buy more washcloths," I offered. "You won't have to do laundry any more often."

Problem solved.

Lessons learned: Sometimes, especially when you are very close to an ugly, challenging problem, you need to consider that the problem might be you. If it is, you would do well to figure out a new way to do what needs to be done that doesn't create more work for everyone else.

Oh yes, and if you have a book to write, make time to write it before you move to the nursing home.

Chapter 7
Progressing from Bad to Worse

August 25, 1986 10:00 a.m.

As plans progressed according to Dorothy's schedule and duty assignments, I had what at one time I had thought might be my last biweekly appointment with my non-orthopedic surgeon who, despite my regular inquiries about prescribing physical therapy, had not yet done so. In spite of the powerful pain pills I continued to lick off the counter, my left elbow was still rating about a 7 on the pain scale of 1-10. The treatment he had employed to apply pressure on my shoulder where the bones were separated, earned the same number if I was in a vertical position. Since the pressure was intended to fix the separation, and since I was not sitting or standing very much due to the pain the pressure caused, I was concerned about whether there was any progress in regard to that injury.

Dr. Non-Orthopedic Surgeon agreed to my request to have an x-ray taken, and at the hospital I asked the technician if I could see the x-ray. She probably broke some kind of rule when she showed me, but there it was—obvious even to me, with no medical knowledge but being smart—that the bone that is supposed to go straight across from your neck to your shoulder so you can hang your shirts there was not straight. There was a cliff right in the middle about an inch high.

Look, Ma! No Hands!

"Hmmm," I said. "No wonder they called it a separation." The technician nodded in agreement.

"My accident was six weeks ago. I wonder what it looked like when it first happened." She broke another rule and pulled out the first x-ray dated July 20.

"Hmmm," I said, aware of the redundancy. "This looks like a carbon copy! There is no change at all!" Horizontal didn't work.

Dr. N-O-S called the next day to tell me that unfortunately, the shoulder was still separated and that the only way to fix it would be surgery, which I presume he thought he would do. Even though I had licked a pain pill off the counter a few hours earlier, I was prepared.

"I want to get a second opinion." I called the orthopedic surgeon who had been on vacation in July. He was able to see me the next day at his office in the town where I lived but where he did not have hospital privileges. Gladys picked up all my x-rays (elbows and shoulder) at the hospital, and took me and the pictures to see him. He looked at the shoulder and all the pictures.

"Well, your shoulder is a mess, and it will require surgery to repair. But I am more concerned about your elbows. Where are the more recent x-rays?"

"There aren't any."

Since I promised not to turn this tale into a medical case study, what follows is, believe me, the short version. New x-rays taken by Dr. No-Longer-On-Vacation Orthopedic Surgeon showed a subluxation in the left elbow. That's a different kind of dislocation than the original injury. Even with no medical knowledge I could

Progressing from Bad to Worse

see that the ulna (the bone that Dr. N-O-S did not remove) had kind of slipped out of the joint. Dr. N-L-O-V-O-S thought perhaps there was instability and the ulna might slip in and out. A subsequent x-ray two days later showed the identical subluxation.

When Dr. N-L-O-V-O-S operated two days later, he found that the elbow had healed with the ulna in this position. The joint was filled with scar tissue and bone fragments from the original injury. Dr. N-L-O-V-O-S cleaned it all out, fit the bones together as well as he could given the absence of the radial head which had been removed by Dr. N-O-S, wrapped up my arm in a new cast and x-rayed it to be sure everything was where it belonged.

It wasn't. There was that subluxation again! Dr. N-L-O-V-O-S removed the brand-new cast, reopened the arm, fit the bones back together, put in several pins to hold them there, and put on a new cast. The surgery that was supposed to take about an hour took four.

The realtor who had sold my house to the first buyer the first day it was on the market volunteered to oversee the movers while they packed up everything that Penny and I had determined should go to Connecticut. I was still in the hospital 14 hours post-surgery with excruciating pain in my left arm and no sensation in my left hand. Thinking swelling had rendered the post-pins cast too tight, Dr. N-L-O-V-O-S had returned to the hospital at midnight the night of the surgery to remove the cast. He put on yet another new cast. After all, they say the third time's a charm right?

Wrong. I spent the next night at a neighbor's

house since mine had been packed up, and Meg and I departed for Connecticut according to Dorothy's schedule the following morning with a prescription for stronger pain pills to be filled as soon as I found a pharmacy in Connecticut.

We checked in at our hotel and called it a day. Tomorrow would be soon enough to find the townhouse I had rented sight unseen in a town I had never heard of but that I had been told was conveniently located between the rural main campus and the Hartford regional campus where I was told I would spend a lot of time. I swallowed two of those powerful pills and fell asleep still unable to feel anything but pain.

We arrived at my new home about 15 minutes before the moving truck the next morning. Meg found the key exactly where we had been told it would be and opened the door. We quickly discovered that the living room was large enough for the baby grand, and the entire house would be quite adequate, at least for my first year in this new state where I didn't know a soul. I took a deep breath just in time to greet the movers.

We walked through the house with the fellow who was obviously in charge, pointing out which beds would go in which bedroom (there were two), which furniture would go in the basement den and what besides the baby grand would remain on the main floor in the living/dining room. I explained that Meg and I would be leaving in about an hour as I had an appointment with the orthopedic surgeon my soon-to-be colleague had convinced to take me as a new patient.

"You will find that the boxes are marked with the

room they belong in, so when you begin unpacking…" he interrupted me. "We don't unpack; we just unload."

"No, that's not right," I said. "I contracted for packing and unpacking."

"Nope," he insisted. "I got two more partial loads to get off the truck before tonight. I don't unpack. That's not what my paperwork says."

"What?" I was incredulous. "Look at me, sir. Do you think I would not have contracted with your company to unpack? I have no hands!"

He paused. "But my paperwork…"

This time I interrupted him. "Call your office now," I insisted. Of course I was right. And he was not happy.

Meg and I left an hour later to meet Dr. Jacobsen who was actually quite excited to have me as a new patient. He, like every other orthopedic surgeon I had met up until that time and every one I have met since, knew that it was impossible to do what I did to both elbows at the same time! I told him, like I have told every other incredulous orthopedic surgeon, that I did not intend to show him how I had done it. Unlike Dr. N-O-S, Dr. Jacobsen set me up to begin physical therapy on Monday and told me I would have daily appointments for many weeks.

Meg and I found a grocery store and bought enough food to get through the weekend figuring Dorothy would be able to shop on Monday. We headed home eager to see what progress had been made. The moving van was gone. Meg opened the door. Everything had been unpacked. And unloaded onto any available flat surface. Every table top, the baby grand, the countertops AND the floors were stacked with dishes, glasses, pots, pans, books, knick knacks, linens, canned goods, cereal, boxes of pasta, rolls of paper towels and toilet paper, and appliances. The seat of every chair and the sofa were piled high. I had paid to move 10,000 pounds of stuff, 8,000 of which had now been unpacked and piled anywhere they could put it other than where it would logically belong.

We stood in the entryway aghast. The powder room to the right was unusable. Stuff filled the sink, and the toilet had served as a linen closet. So much for vomiting, which was what I was feeling an urgent need to do.

Meg looked extremely perplexed. "We can't even walk into the kitchen," she observed. The floor was wall-to-wall glassware; the counters and kitchen table and chairs were piled high. "I don't even know where to put down this bag of groceries!"

"The ice cream is going to melt," I said. "Can you find some spoons? We can sit on the front steps."

Progressing from Bad to Worse

Lessons learned: Even when things are bad, they can get worse. When that happens, sometimes all you can do is find some spoons and a place to sit so you can eat the ice cream before it melts.

Chapter 8
Ten Times Bigger

September 15, 1986 7:30 a.m.

Dorothy assessed the choices hanging in the closet in my new bedroom and took out the fuchsia maternity mumu.

"This color is great on you, Doe. It will work."

While this was not the image I would ordinarily have wanted to portray on my first day as the dean, the choices were limited. She pulled the frock down over my head and arms and picked out some earrings that did nothing to detract from the hot air balloon look I saw in the mirror. She slipped the keds on my feet (when your arms are strapped to your torso and you regularly lick a pain pill off the counter, heels are out of the question).

"Ready?" she asked.

We headed east and began what would be my daily commute. The highway ended and we turned onto Route 6, which I later learned was one of the most dangerous roads in the U.S. Butterflies in my stomach began to activate, not because of the perils of Route 6, but because of what would begin shortly after we arrived at our destination.

I had called for a meeting of all the staff for 10 a.m., giving enough time for the staff who were based at the five regional campuses to travel to Storrs to meet the new dean.

I had, of course, met with the people who would report directly to me during the two visits I had made to the campus as a candidate. Beverly, the dean's administrative assistant, had been so helpful after my accident. Her referral to Dr. Jacobsen was a relief. I was living in the lovely townhouse she had found for me and where I trusted Dorothy would soon find appropriate places to store the many accouterments of my life that still cluttered most of the tables and the baby grand.

The assistant dean had already told me she intended to retire the following year, and the six men who were directors of the various departments were also long-term managers who had been in their positions throughout my predecessor's long tenure. All told, there

were 130 employees in this Division of Extended and Continuing Education. Except for the direct reports who were managerial exempt employees, they all were members of one of five unions represented in the division.

Although the university is a public university partially supported by state funds, most of the division's expenses were paid by fees and tuition for the programs and services provided by the division. These fees paid salaries, benefits, supplies, printing, travel, utilities, equipment, furniture and building renovations.

Ten Times Bigger

As a candidate I had learned that the plan was to move the new dean's compensation from state funding to self support. I successfully negotiated to retain state funding for my position drawing on the principle that as a land-grant university, there is an obligation to serve the out-of-school public and for the university to engage in public service. This was not an optional dean.

During the extensive interview process that included two two-day visits to the campus six weeks apart, I was asked by a member of the search committee if I was ready for this job. He pointed out that it was a much bigger job than any job I had previously held. I responded that it was only ten times bigger—ten times the number of staff, ten times the number of students, a budget ten times larger than the budget at the institution where I was currently the dean.

"A few years ago my husband and I bought a new house, and the mortgage payment was ten times bigger than the mortgage payment on our former home. We knew how to pay the bank."

As I thought about a staff working in six locations, the longevity of the leadership team, the complexities of collective bargaining and five different contracts, the requirement to generate sufficient revenue for all 130 employees to be able to pay *their* mortgage payments to *their* banks, I was already sensing that my response to that question had been naïve or stupid. Maybe both! The search committee was no wiser than I at that moment, and I got the job anyway.

And there I was on my way to my first day at work with no hands. Dressed like a fuchsia hot air balloon in sneakers. Licking pain pills off the counter to try to manage pain I continued to characterize as 7 on that ubiquitous scale of 1-10.

These butterflies were going wild. I remembered when I learned about those butterflies. I was not quite five years old. When my mother had registered me to begin kindergarten, the school administrators suggested that I start in first grade instead. Mother resisted; she herself had graduated from high school at 16 and had not flourished emotionally or socially with her older classmates. They then suggested an out-of-school activity that would be intellectually engaging and challenging (this in the mid 1940s before "gifted education" was incorporated into elementary education). They specifically suggested dramatic lessons as I was highly verbal.

I began taking lessons from Miss Epstein at Junior Theater in a nearby suburb of St. Louis. As I was about to step into the spotlight for the first time in my life, she whispered in my ear, "Dolores, do you feel butterflies in your tummy?"

I did! It felt weird.

"That's wonderful! They are fluttering and fluttering because they are so excited! They know that you know exactly what to do and that you will do it beautifully." With that gift, Miss Epstein defined what others experience as stage fright as something wonderful—my butterflies telling me I am ready. I know what to do and I will do it beautifully. Dorothy pulled the car into the dean's reserved parking spot. My butterflies were going crazy.

Ten Times Bigger

As 10 o'clock approached I could hear the buzz of people moving through the halls to gather in the large training room in the Bishop Center, headquarters for the Division of Extended and Continuing Education that served about 35,000 people every year in credit and non-credit courses and programs, in the university's summer session and in its degree completion program for returning adult students. All 130 staff members who were responsible for those programs had learned about my bicycle accident, that I had injured both my arms and that my starting date had been postponed as a result. While I had communicated with all of them in writing, I knew they would be curious about "the new dean," and would be especially eager to see with their own eyes what she looked like after the accident. This was like stepping into the spotlight to deliver what the audience had come to see.

Miss Epstein whispered in my ear, "Dolores, do you feel butterflies in your tummy?"

The fuchsia hot air balloon entered the room. "Good morning. Thank you for coming today. I have been looking forward to beginning my work here and to meeting all of you. When I scheduled this meeting a few weeks ago, I knew it would be important for you to see with your own eyes that I was here, the accident I had ten days after accepting this position had not had any significant long-term impact, and I was ready to begin the important responsibilities of being your dean."

Look, Ma! No Hands!

I paused for the dramatic irony. "So," another pause..."what did *I* know?" Hmmm. No laughs. The audience didn't get the joke.

"You know that when I ran my bicycle broadside into a moving car, I smashed both my elbows and my right shoulder separated. Surgery was performed to remove the radial head in my left arm, and both arms have been in casts ever since so that these injuries can heal. I learned ten days ago that the left elbow had healed in a dislocated position, and six days ago had surgery to fix that. I am already under the care of a wonderful orthopedic surgeon here in Connecticut, and this afternoon I begin daily physical therapy.

"So while what you see may cause you to wonder, please know that I am indeed here, and I am ready to be your dean. My learning curve will be steep, but I love learning and I am good at it. In addition to the usual challenges any new dean faces, I will obviously have more as a result of the accident and its ongoing complications." I paused again. I searched the room for some sympathetic faces. I made eye contact.

"But I am here, I am ready to be your dean, and I am asking that you believe that I can do all that you expect your dean to do. Please do not be reluctant to ask me whatever needs to be asked. Do not make 'allowances' for me because of limitations you think I may have. I am here and I am ready to be your dean."

I paused again and took a deep breath.

"And the second thing I ask is that you understand if there is something you need, something I should do that I am unable to do right now. Please understand, but please let me be the one to say, 'I'm afraid I can't do that.'"

The room was still. People began to stand. They began to clap their hands and they began to smile.

Lessons learned: Even if it's a bigger job than you have ever had, even if your preparation gets interrupted, and even if you look like a fuchsia hot air balloon, if you have butterflies in your tummy that are telling you that you are ready and you know what to do, you will be able to do it beautifully.

Chapter 9
Tissues, Butterscotch, Hinges and Turnbuckles

October 8, 1986 1:00 p.m.

"Slight change of plans," I told Betsy when she opened the car door for me. "We're not going to physical therapy; Dr. Jacobsen wants to see me in his office."

"Anything wrong?" she asked.

"Yeah. It hurts like hell."

Betsy had answered the ad Dorothy had posted for someone to help me get dressed, run errands, fix some meals and drive me to work in the morning, pick me up at 1:00 and drive me to physical therapy, then take me home, be sure I had dinner that I could manage myself and get me undressed and ready for bed. A young mother of a toddler whose husband was a truck driver and was on the road a lot, she had the time and flexibility. Her daughter Elizabeth enjoyed the ride and often took her afternoon nap during the drive from work to physical therapy.

Betsy enjoyed the adult interaction and conversation, and I was grateful for her cheerful personality and willingness to help. Betsy's employment overlapped Dorothy's last week with me, and the afternoon Dorothy flew home, Betsy took me to Dr. Jacobsen who removed the pins that Dr. N-S-O-V-O-S had inserted to keep the bones in my left elbow in place.

That was two days ago. The pain had begun almost immediately. The physical therapist I saw the next afternoon attributed it to anxiety.

"Your arm has been protected in a cast for two-and-a-half months," she said. "It's not unusual for patients to feel physically vulnerable when that protective cast is removed. Even though you are still in a sling, your arm is exposed. The pain you are feeling is because your brain is saying, 'be careful.'"

That's an interesting theory, but even though I have no medical knowledge, I was smart enough to know that this was a real pain. I still had no feeling in my left hand. If I touched it, it felt like I was touching someone else's hand, but the pain in my hand was still almost unbearable without those pills. This was a different pain, and it was in the elbow, and it was about 8 or 9. She couldn't do much in PT because the pain got worse if she touched my arm.

It was no better the next morning, so I called Dr. Jacobsen as soon as I got to work.

"Let's get an x-ray to see if anything is going on."

He had taken an x-ray just two days earlier before he removed the pins to be sure that the healing was on track so that the pins could be removed. Everything looked fine, so he pulled them out.

I waited in the examination room while the x-ray got developed and read. He came in holding the x-ray and clipped it to a lighted viewing screen so I could see it. I gasped.

"What do you see?" he asked. I saw the subluxation.

Tissues, Butterscotch, Hinges and Turnbuckles

He pulled out the x-rays taken by Dr. N-S-O-V-O-S on September 3 and 5, and in surgery on September 9 after he put on the first cast. The pictures looked like carbon copies. "This explains the pain," he said. My eyes welled up.

"I don't know how to explain the subluxation," he said. "The pins should have stabilized the joint, and they were ready to come out."

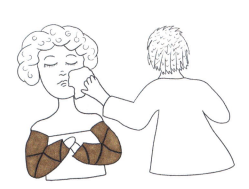

The tears overflowed and rolled down my cheeks. He reached for a tissue and tried to hand it to me. My nose started running, but I couldn't move my arm to reach my nose. He grabbed another tissue and wiped my nose and another one to try to dry my cheeks, but the tears that had been dammed up since July just kept coming.

"Hey Doe, you're a dean. Deans aren't wimps. They don't cry."

"A lot of deans are wimps," I sniffed.

He wiped my nose again. His brow was furrowed. We were both quiet. I sniffed again. He wiped my nose again. Then suddenly he jumped up and opened the door. "Barbara," he called to the nurse, "come here please. And bring some candy. I have to make a phone call."

Barbara took over tissue duty and unwrapped a butterscotch candy and popped it into my mouth. Three candies and a half box of tissues later, Dr. Jacobsen came back. He sat down and spoke quietly.

"I don't know what to do, Doe. An orthopedic surgeon like me will see this kind of injury two or three times in the course of a career, and never bilaterally." I nodded. I knew that you can't do this to both arms.

He continued, "Whatever needs to be done is surgical. I would have the book on elbows open on my lap while I was working on your arm trying to figure out what to do. You deserve better than that. I just got off the phone with Bernard Morrey. He's the man who wrote that book. I want to send you to the Mayo Clinic to see him."

"How do I get an appointment there?"

"I will call him back right now."

Three days later I was in Rochester, Minnesota, with all my x-rays from July 20 to October 8. Dr. Morrey studied them, took some more along with some other tests to measure strength, flexibility and nerve conduction (refuse the latter if you have the choice!). He explained that there was a good chance I would never use my left arm again, and even though there had never been surgery on the right, the delay in starting physical therapy meant that regaining full range of motion in that arm was unlikely. He was also very concerned about my left hand. The loss of sensation indicated that the ulna nerve had been severely damaged or crushed. He proposed a surgical procedure that involved rebuilding the elbow joint using tissue from my thigh to replace ligaments, inserting metal rods through the arm to hold the pieces apart while the soft tissues healed, and after those rods were removed (a second procedure under general anesthesia about one month later), wearing specially designed hinged splints on both arms with turnbuckles that applied constant pressure to straighten the arms.

I would wear these splints 24-7 and would have two special braces for my hand. One would hold the hand straight and the other bent at 90 degrees; I would wear one at night and the other during the day. He projected that I would wear the splints on my arms for two years.

I listened carefully. "Have you ever done this before?" I asked.

"Twenty times."

"Did it work?"

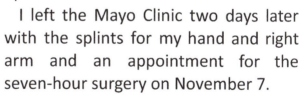

"Eighteen times and I haven't given up on the other two."

I left the Mayo Clinic two days later with the splints for my hand and right arm and an appointment for the seven-hour surgery on November 7.

On November 7 Dr. Morrey found that the ulna nerve had slipped into the joint during the September surgery to insert the pins and was being crushed. He explained that they dissected the nerve and relocated it into fatty tissue in my arm which would provide a better environment for it to heal.

71

Look, Ma! No Hands!

I was skeptical, "Fatty tissue, in *my* arm?"

He smiled. "We had to search but we found some."

I left the Mayo Clinic on November 17 with my arm looking more like a fat roast ready for the rotisserie. On December 18 the four rods that had extended three inches on both sides of my arm were removed, and I went back to Connecticut with both arms in those fancy hinged splints fitted with turnbuckles.

I did indeed wear those splints for two years and became known as the "bionic dean." Dr. Morrey published an article about this procedure he had done 21 times. The second edition of the book on elbows includes a chapter about the procedure. I am pretty sure the photo that looks like a roast ready to go on the rotisserie is my left arm.

Lessons learned: Trust the doctor who knows what he doesn't know. It is okay to cry; and if you are lucky, someone will unwrap some butterscotch candy.

Chapter 10

About Barricades

January 7, 1988 10:30 a.m.

    The sun was warm on my face and outstretched legs. I leaned back against the bench and felt the wind in my face and a salty spray gently brushed against my cheek. As one of Captain Marvin's handsome sons passed out snorkel equipment to the passengers and another son steered the boat toward the Coral Gardens, I recalled an exercise I had participated in many years ago at the beginning of my career as an adult educator. The college where I had just been promoted from Coordinator of Women's Programs to Director of Community Services had sent me to "Management for Women" at the University of Michigan.

    On the final day of the seminar, the professor asked us to write down what we thought we would be doing in five years. We sealed our answers in an envelope and wrote 1979 on the front to remind us to open the envelope that year. I lost the envelope and don't remember what I had predicted, but I know I would have missed the mark by a mile. Never in my wildest dreams would I have predicted that in 1979 I would be a professor myself with the letters Ph.D. after my name, teaching others how to help adults learn and grow.

Look, Ma! No Hands!

Never in those dreams would I have predicted that in January of 1988 I would be on a boat in the North Sound on Grand Cayman with my daughter, Captain Marvin, three of his many sons and a dozen other tourists preparing to snorkel in the Coral Gardens!

Life has a way of happening. My imagination is not creative enough to weave the tales that catapult me forward. I was learning that the plans I invent and the strategies I devise when I land on my feet and catch my breath sometimes get blocked by life. I was beginning to appreciate that what often looks like a barricade can serve as a way to reach a destination that could not be seen, let alone planned for, from my previous perspective. If I can find a way to climb over it or a way to get around that barricade, my new view offers possibilities I could not see or even imagine before.

So in 1985 when I decided that it was time for the tenth dean of adult and continuing education in ten years to move on, that I had done what that college had asked me to do three and a half years before and that I was ready to learn new things in a new place, I resigned in December, effective July 1, 1986. I began the job search that led to my accepting the offer from the University of Connecticut on July 10.

Christmas of 1986 would be my turn to have the kids. Brian would be a junior at the University of South Carolina working toward his degree in Marine Science; Karin would be a freshman somewhere yet to be determined studying fashion buying and merchandising. As I began my job search, I suggested they search for a destination where we would spend the holidays. I suspected that a trip to an exotic vacation spot would be more attractive than being with Mom in a place where she didn't know anyone and neither did they. Brian's top priority was to go somewhere to learn to scuba dive; Karin was looking for a beach and lots of sun. A friend suggested we consider the Cayman Islands, for great diving and one of the best beaches in the world.

I asked, "Where are the Cayman Islands?"

I found them on the map. Having recently transitioned from being part of Jamaica to a colony of Great Britain, Cayman had only recently won its war against mosquitos that were so numerous and vicious they could suffocate a cow. Visionary leaders were in the initial stages of transforming Cayman into the world-class tourist destination it is today. The kids loved the idea.

When I called Brian from Connecticut to tell him I had accepted the job, his immediate response was, "When are you going to make the reservations?" Karin's response was identical.

I went to the travel agent the day I got home, and on July 14 we had reservations for December 22-January 2 in a condo at Island Pines on Seven Mile Beach.

And on July 20 I smashed my elbows.

On October 13 I learned that I would need to return to the Mayo Clinic on November 7 for the third operation on my left elbow, that I would be in the hospital for ten days and would return for a fourth procedure on December 18.

I made an appointment with my superior, the interim provost who had been appointed to fill that role when the provost who had overseen my selection returned to the faculty in September. This was my second meeting with my new boss, and I was there to inform him that in addition to the delay in my start date and my daily physical therapy that had reduced my time at the office to four hours a day at the most, I would be absent for much of November and several days in late December. I was prepared to tell him I would cancel my reservations for a holiday vacation in the Cayman Islands with my kids.

He greeted me warmly and asked how I was doing. It was the perfect opening to share my latest setback. Four weeks and two days into my new job my health situation was getting worse not better. I fought back the tears (deans aren't supposed to be wimps) and tried to matter-of-factly explain how I had become a patient of the man who wrote the book on elbows who thought I might never use my left arm again.

"Well, all I can say, Doe, is that God must have a very high opinion of you! I've always believed He never gives us more than we can handle. So, wow! He obviously believes you are a world class weight lifter." We both laughed, and then he realized his metaphor was particularly inept! We laughed again.

"You need a Jewish mother," he continued. "And I will take that role if you'll have me." I began to wonder if in fact I had died and gone to heaven. "What is the recuperation after the December procedure?"

"Dr. Morrey said I should give myself a week or so to get my strength back, not to expect to hit the ground running. And of course now I will begin the physical therapy on the left arm as well as the right to supplement what the splints do."

He made some notes and looked up. "It seems obvious to me that spending time on the beach is the best way to get your strength back. Under no circumstances are you to change those plans as long as Dr. Morrey approves."

On December 18 Dr. Morrey pulled out the rods, on December 19 I got my left arm splint and flew back to Connecticut. On December 22 I flew to Columbia, South Carolina, where Brian picked me up at the airport, and we drove to Florida and picked up Karin at her college. At 9:30 we boarded a plane in Miami for our first trip to Grand Cayman.

On December 30 Karin and I were walking on Seven Mile Beach, she in her bikini, and I in more dean-like beach attire and of course wearing my fancy splints with the turnbuckles. We noticed a sign almost buried in the sand that said, "Come see our time shares."

One year later, January 7, 1988, Karin and I were with Captain Marvin et al, on an excursion arranged for the timeshare owners at Plantation Village. I left my fancy splints with the turnbuckles in Unit 42 (salt water surely is not good for such equipment) and was ready for the adventure!

Karin helped me put on the fins. I could not straighten my arms enough to reach my feet. I tightened the belt around my waist that would help me stay afloat. Karin stepped off the rear of the boat and dropped into the crystal clear blue water. I watched as she turned face down and swam a few feet from the boat. She returned to the boat, raised her face and gave a big thumbs up as she treaded water waiting for me to step off the boat.

I froze. How deep was this water? Did he say 12-15 feet? What if my arms don't work? Suddenly they ached...at least a five on that scale...and I remember my physical therapist from what seemed like a long time ago telling me that my brain was telling me to be careful...and I was still frozen. Slowly I pulled off my mask waiting for the butterflies to calm down.

Karin pulled her mask off. "What's wrong, Mom?"

"I can't do this."

"What?"

"I said, 'I can't do this. I'm afraid. I don't know if I am strong enough. I just can't."

My daughter swam closer to the boat so she did not have to yell. Calmly she said, "I don't understand. You have always told me that I can do anything I want to do. If I set my mind to it, I will find a way. I have watched you all my life and you have shown me that is true. You make up your mind and you find a way. You CAN do this."

I was afraid...an emotion I do not feel often. My daughter was waiting for me to show her that I can do this if I want to. Miss Epstein whispered in my ear. My butterflies were going crazy.

About Barricades

I took a deep breath and, mask in hand, stepped into the crystal clear blue water that was 15 feet deep.

Lessons learned: Life happens. Believe the butterflies.

Chapter 11
Delusions and Train Wrecks

July 13, 2021 2:00 p.m.

I checked in at the front desk and began to work my way through the stack of forms I needed to complete so that my new primary care physician would have the whole story of my almost 80 years on the planet. I met him a few months ago when Allie, my physical therapist, said the chronic swelling in my feet was contributing to my gait issues. She wanted me to get an evaluation, and since my primary care physician had announced her retirement, I figured this provided a good opportunity to audition a potential new one.

Dr. Goss passed the initial screening. He was taking new patients, was located in the same medical office complex as my physical therapist, and in the same shopping plaza as one of my favorite Mexican restaurants. The fact that he was in the early years of his medical career gave me hope that I would not need to find a new doctor when he retired. I liked the way he listened to my description of the issue that had prompted the visit, and I liked the way he answered my questions. He heard me when I told him that diuretics did not seem to do anything other than force me to walk much faster than was safe or comfortable from my office to the ladies' room down the hall…make that way down the hall. I was pleased that he referred me to a vascular specialist and explained why he thought she might be able to determine why my feet looked like balloons by the end of most days.

When I was leaving, with an appointment already made with the specialist I would see in a few weeks, I informed Dr. Goss that he had passed the audition he did not know he was engaged in. I also told him that this would probably be a long-term relationship since every palm reader who has ever looked at my hand has dropped their jaw and, after raising it again, told me my lifeline says I will live to be 120.

"Which is the lifeline?" he asked. We compared our lifelines; and his, like most people's, ends at his wrist whereas mine curves around the base of my thumb. "Wow, that's really impressive!" he exclaimed.

"Yep. You've got me for the next 40 years."

"I think it's 41."

So here I was for my official transition meeting with Dr. Goss, having now been diagnosed with lymphedema and scheduled to begin lymphedema therapy, also in this same medical office complex, the following week. The specialist had explained that the mechanical system that moves the lymph throughout my body had broken down. She explained that the lymph system collects all the dead cells, toxins and other junk that was not being efficiently eliminated.

"So my feet and legs are being bathed in sewage," I said.

"That's a great metaphor," she said. "I'll remember it because that's a great way to explain it to my patients."

"What caused the system to break down?"

She paused, picked up my file and started reading: "Two Cesarean sections in 1965 and 1968, cholecystectomy in 1967, a separated shoulder and bilateral comminuted fractures of both elbows (*'How did you do that? That's impossible!'*) requiring multiple surgeries on your left elbow in 1986, a laminectomy in 1992, multiple bouts of diverticulitis beginning in 2002, pneumococcal pneumonia in 1979, 1988 and 1993, Parkinson's diagnosed in 2009, spinal fusion in 2013, a broken ankle in 2014 from a fall following six months of severe neuropathy brought on by a paradoxical drug reaction initially begun to treat sciatica prior to the spinal fusion, melanoma removed in 2019 and a squamous cell carcinoma a few months ago, carpal tunnel surgery on your right hand and cubital tunnel in the right elbow also in 2019..." she shook her head. "Doe, your medical record is a train wreck! Your lymphatic system is worn out!"

"Yeah...and that list didn't include the hearing impairment that I've had since 1968—my audiologist says I only hear vowel sounds—and I'm being treated for macular degeneration and get shots in my eyes about every eight weeks. Oh, and the shoulder is still separated. I've been on the list for a body transplant since I smashed my elbows. I like being a girl, and I want to keep my brain. Even with Parkinson's, it's working pretty well! The rest of the parts really need replacement!"

The paperwork for Dr. Goss began with a simple question, "How do you rate your health?"

I checked the box for "Excellent" and moved on to the next question. As I listed the surgeries, the serious illnesses, and the allergies to most antibiotics that have been invented to date, I recalled the characterization of "train wreck." I flipped back the pages, now filled with lots of medical terms I have learned to spell as the list has grown, and amended question #1: "How do you rate your health?" "Excellent, but I may be delusional."

Dr. Goss reviewed that entire list with me; I added details and stories. He closed the file and smiled. "Doe, you are an example of why we cannot practice medicine by reading the files and test results. This file with its surgical notes, lab tests, other scans and x-rays just doesn't match the woman I am talking with. If I didn't know better, I would think they gave me the wrong file."

"I think that's probably a good thing."

He nodded, "You've got that right!"

Lessons learned: Delusions aren't necessarily bad. If your medical record looks like a train wreck but you think you are ok, you just might be…maybe even for 41 more years.

Chapter 12
Puzzle Pieces

During the time that will forever be identified as "The Pandemic," I discovered that assembling 1000 piece jigsaw puzzles helped keep me sane. In an attempt to make up for my disappointment that the Cayman Islands had been closed to tourists since the beginning of the Covid pandemic, Karin had given me three jigsaw puzzles for Christmas in 2020…all beach scenes.

I found working on the puzzles an antidote to pandemic fatigue, a paradoxical way to relax while focusing on accomplishing a task, a positive kind of addiction that lured me from my computer and a seductive attraction that succeeded in engaging me most evenings and weekends when I might otherwise have been joyfully focused on my work that I love so much!

When I am working on a puzzle, I have to keep the big picture in mind even as I focus on the tiniest detail on each piece. Some pieces should be obvious…the red sneakers on the mottled gray and white and blue sand should jump out at me…whereas wide swaths of clear blue sky interrupted only by a shooting star and a faint new moon appearing just after the sun has dipped into the sea seem undefined and even monotonous. There must be several dozen pieces all shades of blue except for those two pieces with the shooting star. And Jiminy Cricket—I don't see anything that looks like that moon. And some pieces that look like the sky might actually be the sea...and the pieces splashed with white...are these clouds or whitecaps brushing the shore? This is complicated...and I can't find those red sneakers!

Some evenings, when I'm grumbling and about to give up, my neighbor, friend, and helper, Sonia, pops in. Sonia walks my sweet dog, does all my housework and wraps my legs every morning in the compression wraps that I must wear every day because of my broken lymph system. Sonia likes puzzles too. She will scan the table, check out the picture, and reach out, pick up three pieces that go with the one I found with the toe of the red shoe and voila! There are the shoes! And the blank space where the moon should be is soon filled in...and I am again motivated to keep at it, emboldened by her clear vision where mine was blurred and confused! Another lesson I learned long ago: Other people can see things I don't, and it's more fun to work together.

I recall working with Ann, my wonderful therapist, nearly 40 years ago, when I decided that life...certainly my life...is a lot like a jigsaw puzzle. But there is one huge difference. Unlike the jigsaw puzzle that came in the box, the puzzle of my life—and yours—didn't come all packaged with a photo on the box to guide us as we put predetermined pieces together. We create that picture ourselves, sometimes with pieces we are given, sometimes with pieces we find along the way.

Puzzle Pieces

The picture evolves, and we have the power to create a picture that will work for us. Part of the fun and the challenge is that we really don't know what the final picture will be until the last piece is put in its place.

Sometimes I get a puzzle piece I didn't ask for, but that I can't discard—like smashing both my elbows in a bicycle accident—and I need to redesign the picture incorporating this intrusive piece. Sometimes I myself choose to include a piece that catches my eye but that complicates the original design...like seeing a sign on the beach that says, "Come see our timeshares."

A favorite sage of mine is known as Emmanuel, and his wisdom is shared in a book appropriately entitled, *Emmanuel's Book*. It is a conversation between him and others seeking to learn from him. Emmanuel tells them that life is like school; we are on this planet to learn what we have forgotten. One man responds to that idea that he must be doing it right because he never liked school, and he's not very happy with his life. Emmanuel tells him that is not the message.

"Whenever the pleasure leaves you, ask yourself 'what have I forgotten?' and if you are in truth, and if you are centered, the answer will be, 'Oh, I forgot…I am the one creating this life. It is in my power to put the pieces of this puzzle together and decide what the picture needs.' I've done a bit of paraphrasing there, but that brings me back to my metaphor.

I embrace the opportunities that come with those unexpected puzzle pieces. I would go so far as to suggest that when we begin putting the puzzle of our lives together, we should not seek the edges first…the edges limit us…establish boundaries that get in the way of our becoming all that we can be. By living within those boundaries, we forget that we have the power to put this puzzle together in ways that bring us joy and bring joy to those we share our lives with even when the pieces we must work with are confusing, frightening, or even painful.

My beach puzzle is almost complete…and at 79, most of the pieces and patterns of the puzzle of my life are easy to see. But I still keep the edges open.

If the palm readers are correct and I live to be 120, that's nearly 41 more years! If I were asked to predict what is yet to come, what pieces and patterns I will put together even in the ten years I have left according to life expectancy data, I know I would likely be wrong. As the whole picture becomes clearer, I begin to see the connections between not only the individual pieces but how the patterns connect to other patterns. As they connect, pattern after pattern, and I step back from the table to get a better view, I realize that this picture could not exist without every single piece that is there. I rarely understand or appreciate the value of each piece at first. I find as I move through my decades that when I first encountered that piece, I did not see how valuable it would be, how without that piece, the picture that is emerging would be very different.

I hear Miss Epstein whispering in my ear every time I feel those butterflies...whether it is stepping up to a podium, walking into a classroom meeting a new class for the first time, calling a meeting to order, or waiting for one of my doctors to define the medical terms on a test result that will explain a new collision in my life so littered with debris of other train wrecks. When I feel those butterflies—that feeling that most people call stage fright that can cause them to break out in a sweat, get dizzy, nauseous and weak kneed—I know that I am ready.

In my first career as a child actress, initially in St. Louis and then in New York City, I learned to pay attention and to listen. Carefully. It was 1947 when I first appeared on television, a technology so new that my father and brother would go to the appliance store in town to watch me. A variety show featuring children, called *Uncle Russ's Family*, was created for the Saturday morning audience, and I became the actress in that family that included another little girl and two little boys who sang and danced. Uncle Russ only let me dance once, and it was clearly conveyed to me that I could not sing, that I was tone deaf. But as the actress, I did most of the speaking, something that even then I was quite good at.

I also was cast as Betsy Carter, the daughter of Jim and Sally, on the Mary Lee Taylor show, a nationally broadcast radio soap opera. I did not yet know how to read, so scripts would be delivered to our house by messenger so that I could memorize them before going live a few days later. Rehearsals were immediately prior to going on the air, and of course, lines would be changed, deleted or added. To this day I have an uncanny recall of dialogue and conversation, I think because when other kids were learning to tie their shoes, I was learning my lines and listening carefully for my cues.

Since I retired from my career in higher education, I have been a teacher of leadership. I truly believe that listening is the most critical of all leadership skills. Before we can speak persuasively and influence others, we need to listen to them, understand their concerns and their feelings, and see their dreams.

When Dr. King Jr. said, "I have a dream," we are moved because his dream is our dream too. He listened carefully and understood us and our dreams. I am grateful that I learned that powerful lesson so early in my life. Of course, I still can't tie my shoes and am also grateful for the invention of Velcro!

We moved to New York the summer before I was eight (by then I could read). My career in St. Louis had been created after my one and only audition; I was the one and only child actress in town. In New York I was one of many. I recall well my first audition there. A ride on the fastest elevator I'd ever ridden in the tallest building I'd ever been in ended when the elevator doors opened, and Mother and I stepped out to join a line of dozens of beautiful little girls in their pastel pinafores. When my turn came, I entered a small room where a kind gentleman asked me to read a few lines of a script.

When I finished, he asked, "Dolores, do you sing?"

Oh dear. I paused; I knew the answer. "Well sir, that's not my profession." Pretty good answer for an eight year old, right? Then he asked me to sing Happy Birthday. I did. I got the job on the Hallmark Hall of Fame, one of four little girls welcoming the Swedish singer, Jenny Lind, to America. I sang, "Oh Jenny Lind, Our Jenny Lind, we bid you welcome, Jenny Lind." My mother often told the story that the director later told her he needed children who sounded like children, not like trained singers!

Why is this piece important to the bigger picture? I think it may be the first time I learned the importance of what we call embracing our vulnerability, of taking a chance and being real. The payoff is authenticity, trust, connection…and maybe even getting to sing on television!

Fast forward. Having decided in junior high school that I didn't want to be an actress anymore, that I didn't want to be different than my classmates, and that I'd rather be a cheerleader than an actress (I never was a cheerleader—I was no better at cheerleading than I was at singing), I graduated from high school and went off to college where I majored in speech and drama with the idea that I might be a teacher.

In the fall of my senior year, one of my professors called me into her office. "Doe, have you thought about graduate school?"

I smiled, "Dr. McCurdy, I am getting married in June."

"I know. But have you thought about graduate school?"

Didn't she hear me? I repeated, "I am getting married."

"Doe, you can do both."

Dr. McCurdy wanted to nominate me for a Woodrow Wilson Fellowship, a national program to prepare people to become university professors in the humanities. After I read the materials and application, I pointed out that students in the performing arts were excluded. She patiently asked me what I would like to study if I did go to graduate school, and when I said dramatic literature and theater history, she grinned. "That's humanities...fill out the application."

She convinced me that signing the statement that said, "I will consider a career in college teaching" was not an untruth and that my intellectual autobiography (I thought I didn't have one) was simply an essay explaining why I was interested in studying dramatic literature and theater history. That was easy for me to write.

I was shocked to be invited to an interview and traveled to Kansas City with two Economics majors who seemed very smart to me. When we arrived at the hotel where the interviews were being held, I looked around the room and was more puzzled about how and why I was there. Only one other girl was in the waiting room filled with smart looking young men, and she also looked pretty smart...wire rimmed glasses, hair in a bun...you get the picture. In 1963, I did not feel or look smart.

I was summoned to the door of the interview room; and before we entered, the chairman (a very smart looking old professor) said to me, "Miss Freedman, I should tell you that we don't give these fellowships in your field." My butterflies began to flutter.

"I know," I said. "I was surprised to be invited today."

"Well, when we read your intellectual autobiography, we thought it would be interesting to meet you."

I GOT IT. I was the comic relief of the day. I mean, hour after hour of interviewing smart economists and historians has got to get pretty dreadful! I relaxed because I understood that role and was ready to play it. I sat at a card table with a pitcher of water and a plastic cup facing an open horseshoe of smart looking old professors, and we had a lovely conversation about a director's responsibility or lack thereof to the original intent of a playwright. I got the fellowship.

This is the lesson of learning not to take yourself too seriously. Providing the comic relief has its place and its rewards.

And yes, I did marry my high school and college sweetheart; yes I did get my master's degree, and I did teach high school speech and English before we started our family. Then I returned to my original vision of my future as wife and mother, that puzzle that I had begun putting together before Dr. McCurdy added an important piece to the puzzle.

And in 1973 after months of marriage counseling and lots of valium prescribed for clinical depression, I gave myself permission to once again take Dr. McCurdy's advice and "do both." At a time when wives who were mothers did not have jobs outside the home, I, a member of the well-behaved "Silent Generation," broke the rules and became the Coordinator of Women's Programs at William Rainey Harper College in suburban Chicago. It was the first women's program in Illinois, and my advisory committee and I created a program that provided enrichment for college educated women so that they would need less valium and marriage counseling. But we also created learning experiences and support systems to facilitate women's reentry to college, to support and strengthen them if they decided to break a rule or two.

Fifteen months later I was promoted to be Director of Community Services. My wise and insightful boss, the Dean of Continuing Education, gave me important advice, a puzzle piece that I now realize is central to the jigsaw puzzle that is my life. "Doe, you are now a company man." Jack winked; I was the only woman at the academic leadership council table.

"So it's important for you to know who you are, what is important to you, your values. Because there may come a day when the company will ask you to do something which goes against those values or that identity. You need to know where to draw the line, because when the company asks you to cross that line, it is time for you to leave. If you don't cross that line, you are no use to the company. And if you do cross it, you are no use to yourself."

I remembered his counsel in December 1985, when I handed my resignation as the tenth dean of adult and continuing education effective July 1, 1986, to the president.

"Where are you going, Doe?"

"I don't know, but Karin graduates from high school in June, so I can go wherever the job search takes me. But I want to be honest with you rather than start looking surreptitiously. You have decided to realign adult and continuing education with the marketing arm of the college, a decision I cannot support.

"We are successful attracting adult learners in such large numbers because of the outstanding academic programs we offer. Continuing education is not marketing; it is and should be aligned organizationally with the other academic programs of the university. This is a disagreement about a core belief and value I hold dear. It is time for me to leave."

July 1 came and went and I still did not know what my next job would be. Then UConn called and I told them I was ready for the job that was only ten times bigger than anything else I had ever done.

And then I smashed my elbows.

Puzzle pieces went flying off the table leaving a huge hole, and pieces that did not look like they would fit anywhere were dumped on the work surface. I needed to find out what I could do with no hands. When I now look at the puzzle from the distance of almost 40 years, I celebrate the way those unwanted pieces made it possible to create the life that I am in love with today.

Look, Ma! No Hands!

    The lessons learned when I had no hands have guided my decisions during what is now the second half of my life. By literally tying my hands, the angels that watch over me gave me no choice but to slow down, watch and listen in my new job that I so naively assured the search committee I knew how to do. Prohibited from jumping in and moving quickly to transform and energize the division I quickly saw needed both transformation and energy, I learned what I did not realize I did not know. By the time I returned from my first trip to Cayman, sporting bilateral fancy splints with turnbuckles, I was able to begin that transformation and lead in new directions and in new ways without making too many mistakes.

    When Tom stepped up to replace me as the parent who would support our daughter as she navigated the first weeks of her autonomous existence 1,396 miles from the home she had known for four years, their relationship found a firmer base. The void created when I smashed my elbows opened a door he might never have tried to open had I been there. And having opened it, his life and Karin's have been enriched.

    I found strength I did not know I had and resilience born of necessity and comprised of humor, humility, self-compassion and a sense of purpose. That resilience has been called on time and time again during the train wreck that is my medical history since I smashed my elbows. That time which the first ten chapters of this book describe was indeed a school where I learned many lessons that have helped me learn and grow and change.

Puzzle Pieces

Lessons learned: There are always lessons to learn. And if we are patient and if we work hard to see it, there will be cause for celebration as the puzzle pieces of our life come together.

Epilogue

Today, 2022

The diagnosis of Parkinson's disease in 2009 was devastating. At the age of 67 I learned that the annoying tremor in my right hand was not the "essential tremor" a neurologist in 2004 believed it to be. It was one of eight symptoms of this progressive movement disorder that I was exhibiting. And even though I am pretty smart, someday my brain will no longer be able to communicate with my body. My neurologist calls Parkinson's a designer disease that presents differently in each of us. And as I learned more about Parkinson's, I decided that it would not define me, that it would be an asterisk in my life like those red shoes on the puzzle beach.

I draw on those lessons I learned when I had no hands. I will focus on what I can do, even as that list gets shorter. I will continue to use the skills I have honed and the knowledge I have accumulated to do my work in life, which I believe is to help others learn and grow and change. I will assert my independence and abilities as long as I can, and I will ask for and accept help from others for things I am unable to do myself. I remind myself often that even if I can no longer do something the way I once did, if I am creative and persistent, I may find that it can be done differently. I am kind enough to allow myself the freedom to accept that it may not be done as well as I would like to have done it, but doing it is cause for celebration. I try to be accountable when the problem is not Parkinson's but is me and my response and reaction to the changes taking place due to this disorder. And I carry a figurative spoon so that I can eat the ice cream when I find it in the rubble of a bad day.

For many years, friends have seen me as someone who makes lemonade—pink lemonade—out of lemons. I am thankful for the perspective that allows me to see possibilities even when the situation seems hopeless to others. I am working on recipes to make lemonade from rocks when the lemons have disappeared from my life.

I have learned that it is okay to cry; and when I cannot wipe my own nose, I now know that the kind person who does will not suffocate me. And when I am afraid I cannot do this—whatever the antecedent of "this" is, and my butterflies begin to flutter, I will remember to trust them and believe that I am ready and I can do this, even if the "this" is accepting that I cannot do it any longer.

Life happens. I will live it fully as long as I can. I will believe the butterflies.

Oh yes, for many years I believed I had a book to write about how I learned these lessons that serve me so well. The butterflies were right. I was ready and made the time to write it now.

Acknowledgements and Gratitude

(And a few more stories!)

In Chapter 3, "Write It on the Wall," my friends expressed some concern that I would not be able to tell stories with no hands. I soon put that concern to rest, and during the six months after I smashed my elbows, I accumulated many stories which I have continued to tell for 36 years. I tell them to friends when we reminisce about the past or talk about times when we were frightened, challenged, sick, inconvenienced, handicapped or disabled.

My stories remind me that I can be strong and inspire others to reframe their fears. I use these stories when I am facilitating expeditions leading to

Acknowledgements and Gratitude

self-discovery among adults in my programs who want to understand themselves better. My stories serve as powerful examples of my definition of leadership—giving the best you have to the work of the group and helping others do the same. And when we need some comic relief, I frequently pull up a tale about that time when I had no hands and found a solution to the problem at hand that resulted in uncontrolled and uncontrollable laughter...and still does.

People have been telling me for years that I should write a book filled with those stories, and now I finally have. As I think about the pieces of this part of the puzzle of my life—the "write a book" part—I want to acknowledge those who nudged, encouraged, and assisted me as I occasionally and sporadically put a few pieces together. I am especially grateful for those who in the last four months have sat down at the table with me, pointed out pieces I would need, and often put them in place for me. We do not, cannot, put our life puzzles together all alone, and I never would have written this book without such cheerleaders, helpers and teachers.

Jane Carroll, my dear friend who someday may decide to write her story, got me started by asking if I would be interested in taking a memoir writing class at the Hartford Public Library with her. I had been diagnosed a few years earlier with Parkinson's and had moved to Hartford when a side effect of my initial medication caused a sleep attack on the highway in rush hour. It was either retire (I was 67) or figure out a way to keep working even if I could not drive the 33 miles to and from my Victorian home I loved in Willimantic.

Acknowledgements and Gratitude

    I never considered retiring; instead I moved to Hartford, bought a condo in the same building as my boss (who is Jane's husband, Ted) and told him if he wanted me to go to work, he could drive me! He did, and soon after I made the move, my medication was changed and I got my car keys back. That move brought Jane into my life as a friend and neighbor, and the first assignment in that memoir class is the Preface to *Look, Ma! No Hands!* My life got busy; I did not complete the class, but over the next couple of years I did write the next several chapters and began to realize that as my Parkinson's progressed, I was drawing on the: "Lessons learned" with some frequency. I had also learned that Jane has an editor's eye combined with her friend's heart and soul; and in the dozen years we have been neighbors, she on the twelfth floor and I on the fifth, I have often run things I have written by her for comments and corrections. So, as *Look, Ma!* entered its final stage of development, I went to Jane to help me make some decisions, like "what name goes on the cover?" I knew she would help me find the right answer.

    As the years went on and as more people nudged me to "write a book" with these stories, I sometimes tentatively mentioned that I had started one. About five years ago I got brave enough to share the preface and four chapters I had written with Dougie Trumble, a graduate of the Third Age Initiative™, the program that I direct at Leadership Greater Hartford. My friendship with Dougie continued after her graduation, and at lunch one day the topic of my book came up. I shared it. She read it and on an annual basis, she would ask if I had

Acknowledgements and Gratitude

written any more.

I am a student of adult education. I believe that "adult education" is a discipline, and studying that discipline prepares one to work with adults as learners differently than other disciplines. As a teacher of adults in many settings and as someone who has lived with the diagnosis of Parkinson's disease since 2009 and with the symptoms since 2004, I realized rather suddenly one day that my own approach to living with this disorder was something I could teach others. Just as suddenly, I was motivated to finish *Look, Ma! NoHands!* In two weekends I wrote the last eight chapters. The next weekend I wrote the epilogue. I called Dougie to tell her it was finished and brought her a copy to read. I asked her to tell me if she thought anyone else would ever want to read it.

I told my neurologist, Dr J. Antoinelle de Marcaida, that I thought a program similar to the Third Age Initiative™ could help Parkinson's patients and their significant others find ways to celebrate their strengths, talents and wisdom and channel them to add meaning and purpose to their lives. Research clearly demonstrates that purposeful engagement adds years to our lives, but a diagnosis of Parkinson's frequently leads those with this condition to narrow the focus of their lives, withdrawing from the world in an effort to keep this condition under control. Dr. de Marcaida's enthusiasm lit the fire under me. While she went on a search for funding to support the development of this innovative approach to treatment, I finished my book.

In May each year I try to get together with Lee and

Acknowledgements and Gratitude

Ginger Erdmann, longtime Leadership Greater Hartford friends and supporters who now split their year between Florida and Vermont. On their spring and fall trips north and south, they spend some time with their daughter, Heidi McCann, in the Hartford region. Ginger was diagnosed with Parkinson's several years ago, a bond she and I share. A year ago in May I told them about the idea for the program that Dr. de Marcaida was excited about. They, too, were enthusiastic. This May I told them the funding was in place, and LGH would soon sign a contract for me to develop the program. And I told them I had completed my book.

"What book?" they asked. They had not heard the stories, so I told them about *Look, Ma! No Hands!*

"Do you have a publisher?" Lee asked. I laughed.

"Of course not. This manuscript has been in my computer half written for ten years. I need to figure out how people self-publish books."

"Our daughter is doing that right now. Her book, *Whatever the Future Holds,* comes out next week."

And that is how Lee and Ginger joined Dougie and her husband Tom in a small group of early readers who offered suggestions ("How about chapter titles?" "A timeline would help," etc.) and encouraged me to tell my story. And that is how Heidi and Green Heart Living Press came into my life and into these pages of gratitude.

Other early readers who became cheerleaders were Mae Maloney, Vincent Xavier, Sandi Coyne-Gilbert, Katy O'Leary, Dayl Walker, Marge Schiller and Toby Gary. My daughter, Karin Davis, read every chapter as it was written and often helped me recall some of the details

Acknowledgements and Gratitude

about that summer in 1986. Jeni Hentschel, who became part of the family when she married Tom, reviewed it with her professional editor's skill.

The team at Green Heart Living Press have taken all this and actually made the book you are holding in your hands, all the while encouraging me and teaching me what I need to know and do throughout the publication process and into the future. Elizabeth Hill, Colleen Brunetti, Jaime Williams, Barb Pritchard and Robin Clare have shared their expertise and their time generously.

When we began discussing my idea that the book would benefit from illustrations, my granddaughter, Courtney Davis, suggested drawings for the chapters as she read them. Courtney is not a trained artist, but has always enjoyed drawing. Her style has a whimsical quality that I realized would be compatible with my writing style and my vision for the book.

Fifteen minutes after I texted her, "Courtney, can you draw any of these?" I received three sketches; and the decision was quickly confirmed by my Green Heart team that we had found our illustrator! And the final touch to Barb's wonderful cover design was Cynthia Lang's beautiful photo of Courtney and me. Having been our family photographer since Courtney was three, I knew Cynthia would capture my pride and our delight in our first book, and she surely did!

I believe I had a good story to tell; this incredible team has transformed it into what I hope others will experience as an engaging inspiration.

Of course I would not have had this story to tell

without all the people who supported me in so many ways when I had no hands. I have named many of them in these pages, but there were many more who made it possible for me to survive with a positivity that those who know me well see as the quality that defines me.

As I recounted that time, I came to appreciate that the foundation that prepared me had been laid in the first 44 years of my life. In Chapter 12 I tell some of those stories, but too many of my early teachers are no longer on the planet. I suspect that they never knew how important they were in the construction of my life; but in the weeks since I completed my book, I have found tremendous joy in reconnecting with those I have found and thanking them.

I believe I have angels who watch over me, and I have no doubt that they were with me on July 20, 1986, as I sped down that hill and smashed into that car. I do believe what I long thought was a disaster that I simply had to survive and get past was a gift to me, an incredibly powerful opportunity to learn and grow. I was ready to learn and grow even more when I received my diagnosis in 2009. Today I finally understand that living with Parkinson's has been another gift. I am called on to use everything I know and know how to do, and do it better than I have ever done it so that others can learn to continue building the puzzle of their lives with a purpose, lives in which Parkinson's is an asterisk. My angels have shown me my purpose, and my butterflies are telling me I am ready. I thank them every day.

Books Referenced

I referred to three books in *Look, Ma! No Hands!* each of which is a special part of my story.

And Ladies of the Club

And Ladies of the Club, an engaging historical novel written by Helen Hoover Santmyer (originally published in Columbus, Ohio: The Ohio State University Press, 1982) is a delightful history of a group of women covering many decades of their lives. Santmyer (1895-1986) began writing this novel in the early 1930s but did not complete it until 1976. The Ohio State University Press required significant abridgement, and most of that writing was done while the author was in a nursing home. A few hundred copies were sold, but it was discovered by someone in Hollywood who saw its potential. The second publication by Putnam in 1984 was selected by the Book-of-the-Month Club and the paperback edition by Berkley Books (1985) sold two million copies—the best selling paperback in history at the time. Santmyer spent the last five years of her life in the nursing home and passed away before the popularity of the book, her fourth novel and the primary source of her literary reputation, peaked.

I loved this book and devoured it during the first weeks after my accident. Santmyer had died five months before I read it, and the irony that her last book was the one to bring her fame, made an impression on me. Santmyer had a lifetime of health challenges and finally succumbed at the age of 90. My health challenges are different from hers, and the palm readers tell me I will live to be 120, but as I approached my 80th birthday, I was reminded of Helen Hoover Santmyer and decided it was time to finish my first book. It may never be selected as the Book-of-the-Month by any club other than my own book club, but I am feeling just as proud as I hope Helen did when she completed…Ladies.

The Elbow and Its Disorders

The "book on elbows" is officially entitled *The Elbow and its Disorders*, and the man who wrote it in 1985 is Dr. Bernard Morrey. The book is now in its fifth edition, and Dr. Morrey, emeritus chair of the Department of Orthopedics at the Mayo Clinic, holds the rank of Professor of Orthopedics at the Mayo Clinic and at the University of Texas Health Sciences Center in San Antonio. A year younger than I, he too is still working, undoubtedly making it possible for people like me to resume their lives with elbows that work again. I am forever grateful that he finished the first edition a year before I smashed my elbows. I am indebted to my angels and to Beverly Salcius who connected me with Dr. Wells Jacobsen, who is the hero in my book. Dr. Jacobsen had already read Dr. Morrey's newly published book when I began to cry. As he wiped my tears and my nose, he knew to call the man who wrote the book on elbows, a decision that made it possible for me to continue creating this life with two hands and elbows that work.

Emmanuel's Book

Emmanuel, whose wisdom is compiled by Pat Rodegast and Judith Stanton in *Emmanuel's Book* (New York: Random House, 1987) has helped me understand myself, the course of my life, and the world of my experience ever since my friend, Mary Carey shared her copy of that book with me. I believe Emmanuel when he tells us that "Joy is the God within you, standing up, shaking himself off and beginning to smile." Emmanuel reminds me that it is my responsibility to create this life and to learn in the process. He has given me permission to dance and to sing, even if I make mistakes when I do, because I do not need to get it right in this lifetime.

You may not be interested in Helen Hoover Santmyer's story about the Ladies of the Club, and none of us needs to read Dr. Morrey's book on elbows as long as our doctors do, but if by chance you find that some of the lessons I learned when I had no hands make sense to you, you will very likely find that you can learn from Emmanuel, a much easier way to learn than by smashing your elbows.

About the Author

Doe Hentschel doesn't follow the crowd. Hardly an iconoclast, she has nonetheless blazed a trail unlike most of her contemporaries. A professional actress before she could read, she graduated from high school at 16 and college at 20. The recipient of a Woodrow Wilson Fellowship at 21 and with her Masters in Speech in hand, she taught high school for one year before bringing Brian and Karin into the world. In 1973, guided by a boundary-breaking book, *How to Go to Work When Your Husband Is Against It, Your Children Aren't Old Enough, and There's Nothing You Can Do Anyway* by Felice N. Schwartz, Margaret Schifter, and Susan S. Gillotti, Doe began her career as an adult educator.

When "Dr. Doe" retired at the age of 58 to be a hands-on grandma to Matthew, the first of her four grandchildren, she had served at nearly every type of institution of higher education and climbed the administrative ladder from coordinator to director, to dean and vice president. As a professor, she taught courses in Adult Learning and Development, Continuing Professional Education, Program Development and Implementation, Program Evaluation, Leadership for Change, and Group Dynamics and developed and facilitated internship programs for graduate and undergraduate students.

Doe began her post-retirement career in community leadership in 2000 to develop the Third Age Initiative™, Leadership Greater Hartford's program to identify, develop and engage older adults in meaningful ways in the community. As her grandchildren grew, her career expanded. As Vice President, she led innovative program development and built a robust portfolio of training and consulting programs and services for LGH. Twenty-two years later, as Leadership Preceptor and at the age of 80, she has no plans to retire again.

A teacher in her core, as a dean and vice president, Dr. Doe was also in the classroom. At Leadership Greater Hartford, she teaches, trains, facilitates and coaches learners as they travel along their lifelong leadership journeys.

Doe holds a BA from the University of Missouri-Columbia, MA from Northwestern University, and Ph.D. from the University of Wisconsin-Milwaukee. She has been recognized with many awards over the course of her lifetime including the Preceptor Award from the Association of Leadership Programs, its highest recognition. In 2013, Dr. Doe Hentschel was inducted into the International Adult and Continuing Education Hall of Fame. She has published more than 50 articles, chapters, and research papers. *Look, Ma! No Hands! Life's Lessons Learned the Hard Way* is her first book.

About the Illustrator

Courtney Davis has always had a creative side and at an early age participated in a youth art program where she experimented with all types of media; her favorite was drawing. Courtney also loves to write creative stories. In 4th grade she earned a perfect score on her CT Mastery Test writing exam and won her school's Golden Pen Award. Following her grandmother's example, she has had many jobs in her young life. She has been a scare actor at a local haunted house, worked retail, scooped ice cream, and for the last two years has been a daycare provider at the local day care center in her hometown of Preston, Connecticut. An honor student at Norwich Free Academy, Courtney is currently a sophomore at Eastern Connecticut State University with a double major in Early Childhood Education and Sociology.

Her freshman year she earned an A in an art class in which she was the only student not majoring in art. Having illustrated her first book, she may create the words as well as the drawings for her next one!

Green Heart Living Press publishes inspirational books and stories of transformation and healing, making the world a more loving and peaceful place, one book at a time. You can meet Green Heart authors on the Green Heart Living YouTube channel and the Green Heart Living Podcast.

www.greenheartliving.com

Made in the USA
Monee, IL
09 February 2023